Hearing

CHELSEA
CLUBHOUSE
An Imprint of Chelsea House Publishers
A Haights Cross Communications Company
Philadelphia

Kimberley Jane Pryor

For Nick, Ashley and Thomas

This edition first published in 2004 in the United States of America by Chelsea Clubhouse, a division of Chelsea House Publishers and a subsidiary of Haights Cross Communications.

Chelsea Clubhouse
1974 Sproul Road, Suite 400
Broomall, PA 19008-0914

The Chelsea House world wide web address is www.chelseahouse.com

Library of Congress Cataloging-in-Publication Data

Pryor, Kimberley Jane.
  Hearing / Kimberley Jane Pryor.
  p. cm. — (The senses)

  Includes bibliographical references and index.
  Contents: Your senses — Your ears — A message to your brain — Sound waves — All kinds of sounds — Hearing danger — Hearing loss — Deafness — Protecting your ears — Using all your senses — Glossary.

  ISBN 0-7910-7554-0
  1. Ear—Juvenile literature. 2. Hearing—Juvenile literature. [1. Hearing. 2. Ear. 3. Senses and sensation.] I. Title. II. Series.
  QP462.2.P79 2004
  612.8'5—dc21

                                                                            2003001173

First published in 2003 by
MACMILLAN EDUCATION AUSTRALIA PTY LTD
627 Chapel Street, South Yarra, Australia, 3141

Associated companies and representatives throughout the world.

Copyright © Kimberley Jane Pryor 2003

Page layout by Raul Diche
Illustrations by Alan Laver, Shelly Communications
Photo research by Legend Images

Printed in China

Acknowledgements
Cover photograph: children talking, courtesy of Photodisc.

Jean-Michel Labat/Auscape, p. 21; Eyewire, p. 24; Getty Images/Image Bank, p. 16 (top right); Getty Images/Stone, p. 29; Getty Images/Taxi, pp. 4, 12, 14, 23; Great Southern Stock, pp. 5, 7, 19, 28; Bill Belson/Lochman Transparencies, p. 16 (bottom right); Len Stewart/Lochman Transparencies, p. 16 (center right); Nick Milton, pp. 6, 15; Photodisc, pp. 1, 10, 13, 16 (top, center, and bottom left), 18, 20; Photolibrary.com/SPL, pp. 9, 26; Terry Oakley/The Picture Source, pp. 17, 22, 25, 27.

While every care has been taken to trace and acknowledge copyright, the publisher tenders their apologies for any accidental infringement where copyright has proved untraceable. Where the attempt has been unsuccessful, the publisher welcomes information that would redress the situation.

Please note
At the time of printing, the Internet addresses appearing in this book were correct. Owing to the dynamic nature of the Internet, however, we cannot guarantee that all these addresses will remain correct.

Contents

Your Senses

You have five senses to help you learn about the world. They are hearing, sight, smell, taste, and touch.

You listen to stories with your ears.

Hearing

You listen with your ears. Your sense of hearing helps you learn from other people and enjoy laughter and music. It also warns you of danger.

Your ears tell you that this leaf blower is turned on.

Your Ears

Your ears have three parts:

⚙ the outer ear
⚙ the middle ear
⚙ the inner ear.

The outer ear is made up of the **pinna** and the ear canal. The pinna is the part you can see. It acts as a funnel to collect sounds. Sounds travel down the ear canal.

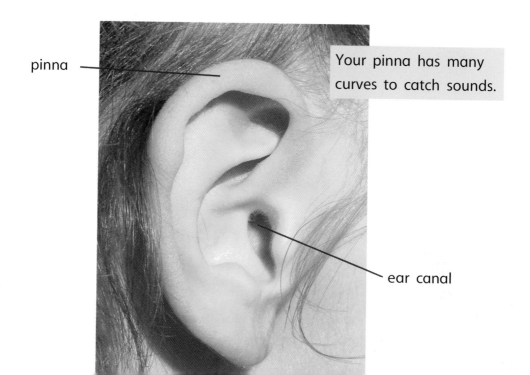

pinna

Your pinna has many curves to catch sounds.

ear canal

You can carefully wipe away earwax with a clean cloth.

The ear canal protects the ear by making earwax. Earwax has special chemicals that fight infections. Earwax also traps dust and dirt. Earwax slowly moves toward the ear opening, where it can be wiped off.

The middle ear is separated from the outer ear by a piece of thin skin called the eardrum. The middle ear contains three ear bones:

✪ the **hammer**

✪ the **anvil**

✪ the **stirrup**.

They are the tiniest bones in the body.

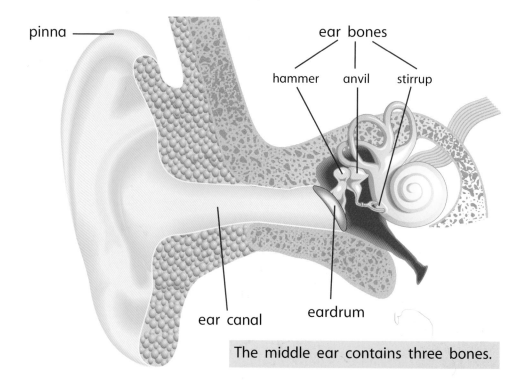

The middle ear contains three bones.

When sounds hit the eardrum, the eardrum begins to **vibrate**. The vibrations move from the eardrum, through the chain of ear bones, and to the inner ear.

The eardrum is very thin. Sounds make it vibrate.

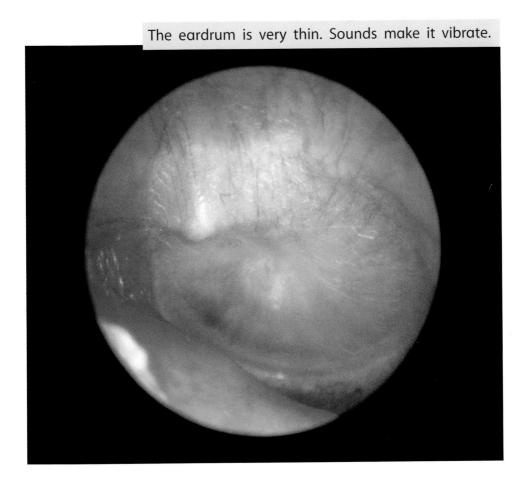

The inner ear contains the **cochlea** and the **semicircular canals**. The cochlea is a snail-shaped tube filled with liquid and lined with hair cells. It lets you hear sounds. The semicircular canals sense movements of the body. They help you keep your balance.

The semicircular canals in your inner ear signal your brain when you are spinning around.

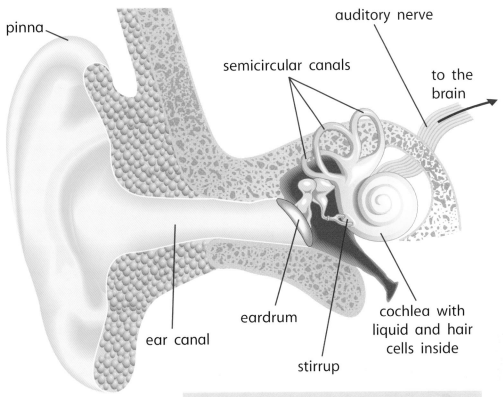

pinna

auditory nerve

semicircular canals

to the brain

eardrum

ear canal

cochlea with liquid and hair cells inside

stirrup

Hearing takes place when hair cells sense vibrations and signal the brain.

When the stirrup bone moves, it makes the liquid inside the cochlea vibrate. This motion makes some of the hairs on the hair cells vibrate. These hair cells send signals along the **auditory nerve** to the brain.

A Message to Your Brain

Once hair cells in your ears send messages to your brain, your brain decides what the sound is. It decides what is making the sound and whether you should do something about it.

Your ears send messages to a special part of your brain.

touch

taste

hearing

smell

vision

When you hear the morning school bell, your ears send a message to your brain. Then your brain sends a message to your feet and legs to tell them to walk to your classroom.

When your ears hear the bell ring, you know you should go to your classroom.

Sound Waves

Sound is made when objects vibrate. A vibrating object sends out invisible vibrations that travel through the air. These invisible vibrations are called sound waves.

When you hit a drum, the drum head vibrates to make the sound.

Try this!

Ask a parent or teacher for help.

Say "ahhhhhhh"

⊗ Place your fingers gently across the front of your throat.

⊗ Say "ahhhhhhh".

⊗ Feel the vocal cords in your throat vibrating to make the sound.

You send out sound waves when you talk, shout, or sing.

Your vocal cords vibrate when you talk.

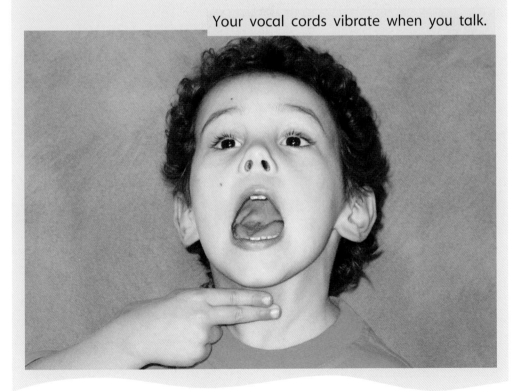

15

All Kinds of Sounds

There are many kinds of sounds. Some are loud and others are soft. The loudness of a sound is called its volume. When someone whispers you may need to lean forward to hear them better. To stop loud sounds from hurting your ears you may want to cover your ears with your hands.

Pleasant Sounds		**Unpleasant Sounds**	
friends talking		person shouting	
bird singing		cat hissing	
music		chainsaw	

Try this!

Make a megaphone

⭐ 1. Roll a sheet of thin cardboard or thick paper into a funnel shape.

⭐ 2. Stick the outside flap down with tape.

⭐ 3. Hold the narrow end of the funnel to your mouth.

⭐ 4. Talk into the **megaphone**.

The megaphone causes sound waves from your voice to travel forward only, not out to the sides. This makes your voice seem louder.

High and low sounds

Some sounds are high, such as the ringing of a small bell. Other sounds are low, such as thunder. The highness and lowness of sound is called its pitch. Bigger objects usually make lower sounds and smaller objects usually make higher sounds.

The bigger the instrument, the lower the sound.

Try this!

Ask a parent or teacher for help.

Mystery sounds

⭐ Collect different objects, such as keys on a key ring, a bell, some coins, a horn, and a ball.

⭐ Ask a friend to close his or her eyes and to listen to each sound as you make it.

⭐ After you make each sound below, ask, "Do you know this sound?"

- shake the keys
- clap your hands
- ring the bell
- blow the horn
- jingle the coins
- bounce the ball

⭐ Can your friend guess what each sound is?

Do you know this sound?

Sudden and ongoing sounds

Some sounds are sudden, such as the slam of a door. Other sounds are ongoing, such as the roar of a waterfall.

There are sounds all around you.

Try this!

Ask a parent or teacher for help.

Outdoor sounds

⭐ Take a notepad and pencil outside.

⭐ Find a place to stop and listen.

⭐ Write down all the sounds you can hear.

⭐ Can you hear leaves rustling or birds singing? Can you hear people, cars, or airplanes?

How many different sounds can you hear?

Hearing Danger

Your sense of hearing helps warn you of danger. When you hear an ambulance siren, a signal goes to your brain and tells you to watch out for a fast-moving vehicle.

People move out of the way when they hear an ambulance siren.

When you hear a dog growl, your brain tells you the dog is angry.

A growling dog may be dangerous.

Hearing Loss

Many people have hearing loss. It may be caused by too much earwax in the ear canal or by a middle ear infection. A doctor can treat these problems and make sure the hearing loss isn't permanent.

Doctors can help children with ear infections.

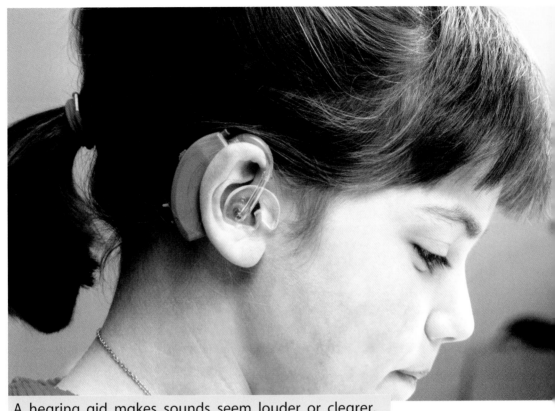

A hearing aid makes sounds seem louder or clearer.

Some people need hearing aids to help them hear better. Hearing aids are worn inside and behind the ear. They make sounds around you seem louder.

25

Deafness

People who are deaf have very little or no hearing. Some people are born deaf. Some people become deaf because they have had a disease, an injury, or repeated ear infections that damage the eardrum.

This child is having her hearing tested.

Some people who are deaf **communicate** with each other using sign language. They use their hands to "speak" and their eyes to "listen". Some people who are deaf can also read lips to know what people are saying.

These children are using sign language to communicate.

Protecting Your Ears

Your sense of hearing is important and helps you learn about the world. So, protect your ears to keep them healthy!

- ✪ Never put sharp objects into your ears.
- ✪ See a doctor if your ears are hurting.
- ✪ Turn down the volume on your stereo and television.

Keep the volume on your headset low to protect your hearing.

Workers who use loud machinery must wear ear protection.

You can protect your ears from loud sounds by wearing earplugs or ear protection when you:

⭐ go to see a band or a concert
⭐ use or stand near loud machinery.

Using All Your Senses

You need your senses to hear, see, smell, taste, and touch things. The best way to learn about the world is to use all your senses.

Did You Know?
You can tell which direction a sound comes from because you have two ears. The ear nearest to the sound hears the sound first and more loudly.

Did You Know?
Owls have excellent hearing to help them find prey. When an owl is flying, it can hear a tiny mouse running in the grass.

Did You Know?
A mother knows her baby's cry, even when her baby is with other babies.

Glossary

anvil	the second of three bones in the middle ear that move vibrations from the eardrum to the inner ear; the hammer moves the anvil, and the anvil moves the stirrup.
auditory nerve	the nerve that takes messages from hair cells in the ears to the brain
cochlea	a coiled tube in the ear that is filled with fluid; the cochlea receives sound vibrations from the ear bones.
communicate	to share information, ideas, or feelings with another person
hammer	the first of three bones in the middle ear that move vibrations from the eardrum to the inner ear; the eardrum moves the hammer, and the hammer moves the anvil.
megaphone	a funnel-shaped instrument used for making voices louder
pinna	the part of the ear on the outside of the head; the pinna has many curves and ridges to funnel sounds into the ear canal.
semicircular canals	three fluid-filled, loop-shaped tubes in the ear that signal movements of the head to the brain and assist with the body's sense of balance
stirrup	the third of three bones in the middle ear that move vibrations from the eardrum to the inner ear; the anvil moves the stirrup, and the stirrup moves a thin, skin-like portion of the cochlea.
vibrate	to move back and forth quickly

Index

Web Sites

You can go to these web sites to learn more about the sense of hearing:

http://www.kidshealth.org/kid/body/ear_SW.html

http://www.brainpop.com/health/senses/hearing/index.weml